The Listening Activity Book

The Listening Activity Book

Teaching Literal, Evaluative, and Critical Listening in the Elementary School

Charlene W. Smith

California State University
Fresno, California

David S. Lake Publishers
Belmont, California

Acknowledgement is made to *Instructor* (The Instructor Publications, Inc., Dansville, New York) which published portions of this material in the article, "Huh? Wadja Say? Index to Better Listening," by Charlene W. Smith (*Instructor*, vol. 84. no. 2, October, 1974, pp. 59-68).

Edited by Lesley Anne Swanson

ISBN-0-8224-4304-X
Library of Congress Catalog Card Number: 75-17340.
Printed in the United States of America.

Contents

Introduction

Spoken words are all around us. We hear hundreds and thousands of them each day, yet knowing how to listen to them is an art. Words can be art or information, casual or formal, vocation or recreation. The reasons for reading and for listening are closely related. Sometimes we listen or read for relaxation and enjoyment. Sometimes our goal is to follow directions. And on other occasions, we must practice critical reading or listening in order to evaluate and make a judgment. But here the similarity ends. While reading is an integral part of the school curriculum, listening is not.

At the elementary level, listening is sometimes emphasized during a story hour when the teacher reads aloud to the class. Some days, the teacher can feel the intense involvement of the entire class as they listen to a suspenseful moment, a rollicking episode, or a somber turn of events. At the best of times, they are all ears. But every teacher has those other days, too, when even during a well-planned lesson, some children simply aren't listening. There are numerous reasons for this. Perhaps they didn't eat breakfast, had an argument on the way to school, are incubating the measles, feeling misunderstood, or just plain daydreaming. Nevertheless, techniques are available to help children learn how to listen (barring the measles problem). One of the teacher's responsibilities is the provision of directed listening experiences throughout the school year. Especially in the elementary school, a program of listening instruction is of prime importance.

Helping children learn to listen for a variety of reasons has a motivational as well as instructional basis. As the teacher introduces a new item or helps children see a previously learned concept in a new light, she is opening up new vistas for the children. Setting the stage for embarking on a new unit, learning about some new library books that have just arrived, listening to find out how a new learning station is to be used are all ways of getting children interested in school.

Once she realizes the need for a regular program of this sort, the teacher should consider these three points:

1. Teachers tend to talk too much. Do we "turn off" children

with too much verbiage? How much is "too much" repetition of directions and instructions?

2. Children need to participate as both speakers and listeners in classroom interaction. Do our attitudes encourage children to contribute? Are we interested listeners ourselves?

3. Systematic experience in learning to listen for specific reasons needs to be explored in elementary classrooms. Helping children understand why they should listen is important. Short, specific practice exercises with content the children find interesting need to be developed for classroom use.

This book contains a variety of practice exercises for you to use with your class, and it explains how you can devise additional exercises to meet the specific needs of your students. Part 1 presents ten basic types of listening experiences. In Part 2, you'll find several listening games for young children. Advertisements are used to teach listening for evaluation in Part 3. And in Part 4, students gain experience in listening to interpret a speaker's motives.

Before you begin, you'll need to set up some standards for behavior during these listening sessions. If the children are old enough, it's best to have the class help you with this task. Some points you'll want to consider are interruptions, talking, walking around, and playing with toys. Once the standards are established, remind the children of them often so they realize you place a high value on good listening habits. Remember, too, to keep these sessions brief and to alternate them with other activities. If the content is intriguing and if they have something to listen for, they'll tune in to what you have to say.

As a teacher, you, too, will benefit from listening instruction. First, you will be encouraged to consider the phrasing of directions in all content areas and in all classroom activities. You may even want to tape record several typical sets of directions, then play them back for yourself to find out just how you sound to the class. Second, you will find yourself listening more intently to the children's comments and questions, thus gaining additional insight into their problems and their ideas.

While environmental factors of physical setting require consideration in providing the best possible listening situation, the teacher must remember that he himself is part and product of a set of factors, an environment. Seeking to listen objectively to children, the teacher recognizes his own prejudices, attitudes, beliefs, and moods. Ideas that are brought to school by the children, language usage, and vocabulary may all be factors that cause the teacher to miss the import of children's comments (similar to the situations when the children *tune out* the teacher) because a topic is not understandable or because there is a deficiency of vocabulary background. A teacher with sensitive receptive abilities is one who encourages oral language and who listens when the children talk. [1]

Extended listening experiences also encourage children to listen to other children, thus broadening the field of classroom interaction from straight teacher-to-students one-way communication to multiple combinations that work both ways. Your development of a classroom that is conducive to listening awareness will be a room which encourages children to be "talkers" and partners in the learning process.

How to Prepare a Listening Experience

There are many reasons for listening in this oral-aural world of ours. Basic to all of them, however, are objectives that need to be considered in developing a planned program in listening instruction at the elementary level. Teaching for good listening requires a program with listening objectives well-defined and listening experiences designed to fulfill them. The behavioral objectives for a typical listening program might read as follows:

Commensurate with individual development and past experiences in listening, children shall demonstrate progressive abilities in the following listening skills:

Noting specific details

Detecting sequence

Noting irrelevancies

Understanding the main idea

Following directions

Making inferences

Predicting outcomes

Evaluating advertisements

Evaluating a speaker's point of view.

---

[1] Williard F. Tidyman, Charlene Weddle Smith, and Marguerite Butterfield, *Teaching the Language Arts*, 3rd ed., (New York: McGraw Hill Book Company, 1969), pp. 80-81. Quoted with special permission of the publisher.

In planning a listening experience, you'll need to pinpoint the objective, then either select or create an appropriate and appealing story. Most crucial are the directions that you next prepare to introduce the selection to the listeners, for it is in these few, brief sentences that the purpose of the listening activity is stated. A discussion period follows each listening experience in which the students answer the questions raised at the beginning. You will also want to evaluate the responses of each child in the listening group and note his level of attainment. Anecdotal records are recommended for this purpose. These will enable you to plan for regrouping, if necessary, and for future listening experiences to meet individual needs. Thus each lesson is composed of five parts: objective, directions, listening experience, discussion, teacher evaluation.

Charlene W. Smith

Part 1
Ten Basic Listening Experiences

The titles of these ten listening selections represent ten types of listening experiences. With a little thought, you can readily develop a number of additional stories to fit each one. Textbooks, newspapers, magazines, and your imagination are all good sources of stories. For example, factual passages from science or social studies texts lend themselves readily to "Private Eye." A funny, unrelated word introduced unobtrusively into a narrative becomes "Silly Sentence." Statistical information can be used in "Tall Tale." Variations on "Tasty Story" might include listening for words about colors, sounds, movements, or emotions. Read a story the children haven't heard, leave off the ending, and you have "What Happens Next?" "Word Picture" prepares students for following directions by impressing upon them the importance of listening for details. You might write up a general and a specific description of an everyday object—a coffee mug, for example—bring several different mugs to class, and ask the students to pick out the one you described.

While large group listening experiences help unify a class, most of the discussion will be carried on by the group's more outgoing members. To encourage the children who are less inclined to speak up, and to meet the needs of children who have specific listening problems, small group work will be a necessary adjunct to your listening program.

These ten listening experiences lend themselves readily to individualizing small group instruction. If some children are having difficulty summarizing information, give them additional practice with "What's the Big Idea?," "Headline," and "Title Me, Please." Encourage quiet children to participate in small groups by having them tell "What Happens Next?" The possibilities are endless. Once middle-grade students become familiar with the types of selections in this section, they may want to create their own listening lessons to present to their classmates.

1 Word Picture
Listening for visual imagery

Directions: Listen carefully as I read two descriptions of one house. As you listen, decide which description gives you more information about the house. Which description would help you recognize the house if you saw a picture of it?

1. Once there was a house in the country. It was far from town.
2. Once there was a little house in the country that stood far from town. The house was white, and it had four windows in the front. The friendly door was painted blue. There were flowers of all colors growing around the house, and many green fir trees grew in the yard.

Discussion:
Evaluation:

2 Tasty Story
Listening for details about taste

Directions: Today I'm going to read a short story to you about Jim and Mike who went to a carnival. Almost everyone gets hungry and thirsty at a carnival, so as I'm reading, you listen for the things the boys ate and drank. When I finish, we can all talk about the different tastes the boys had that day.

As Jim and Mike walked down the midway at the carnival, they realized they were thirsty. Mike stopped by a stand and said, "Hey, Jim! Let's get an orange drink. All this dust blowing around is really bothering my throat."

"Good idea," agreed Jim. They paid for the drinks, lifted their glasses, and let the sweet orange liquid run down their throats.

"Mike," said Jim, "Do you know that it's after two o'clock and we haven't had any lunch?"

"I just saw a hot dog stand over by the Ferris wheel," replied Mike who was just finishing his drink. "They have hot dogs and buns. And on the counter, I saw dishes of pickle relish, chopped onions, mustard, and ketchup. Let's go have a hot dog with everything on it!" Jim didn't answer. He was already running over to the hot dog stand with Mike close behind.

Discussion:
Evaluation:

3 *Silly Sentence*
Listening for irrelevancies

Directions: Here is a story about a boy named Kevin who started out for school one morning. As I read this story, listen for one sentence that couldn't possibly make sense. Remember that sentence so you can tell me what it is when I finish reading.

Kevin had many things in his hands and pockets as he walked to school on Monday morning. His lunch money jingled in his pocket beside his three favorite marbles. In one hand, Kevin carried his grandfather's house. In the other hand, he carried a box where he kept his pet frog, Tiny.

Discussion:
Evaluation:

4 *Tall Tale*
Listening to focus on facts

Directions: Today we have a short story about tall trees called sequoias. Listen carefully while I read this article to you. You will hear many facts about these giant trees, but listen particularly for examples of how big one log of a sequoia can be.

In the western part of our country there are vast forests. In these forests grow some giant trees called sequoias. These trees are tall and very big around. In fact, one of these trees may be as big around as a room in your house. One log makes a heavy load for a truck. Often just one log has wood enough to build five or six houses. The sequoias are hundreds of years old. They started growing long before towns and cities were built in the West.

Discussion:
Evaluation:

5 *Headline*
Listening for the main idea

Directions: Listen carefully as I read a short article about a highway. As you listen, think of a headline that would fit this story if you read it in the newspaper.

Tomorrow a new 50-mile highway will open between Fairfax and Riverdale. People will be able to drive from city to city much more safely now. The new highway takes out a dangerous curve in the old highway and bypasses the old cattle crossing.

Discussion:
Evaluation:

6 *What's the Big Idea?*
Listening for the main idea

Directions: Today you're going to hear an article about the weather all year 'round. As I read, listen carefully and see if each of you can give us a one-sentence summary of the article when I finish.

Some people say that we can't do anything about the weather but talk about it. Do you think that's right? Do you listen to the weather news on the radio or the TV so you'll know what to wear the next day? Will it be a T-shirt or heavy jacket, sandals or rainboots?

Weather stations across the United States send out valuable news bulletins to farmers who want to know the best time for planting their crops. Forest lookouts send out danger bulletins when the woods are dry and no rain is forecast. News about high winds, tornadoes, or hurricanes are broadcast to people living in danger areas.

Weather bulletins about snow conditions help alert people who are in danger of being snowed in. Snow bulletins also help skiers pick the best snow pack for a weekend of sports.

Discussion:
Evaluation:

7 Title Me, Please
Listening for the main idea

Directions: Here is a short story about Lori who was reading a book. As I read the story, you think of a title for it.

Lori was reading a book about the North American Indians. As she read, she tried to imagine what it might have been like in the days before the new settlers arrived in this country. Lori looked out of the window and tried to imagine that she saw no houses, stores, or paved streets. Suddenly she thought she saw trees standing where the buildings used to be. A grassy meadow took the place of streets and sidewalks. A doe and her fawn ran through the meadow and disappeared into the woods. Two Indian boys, laughing breathlessly, raced after the deer.

Discussion:
Evaluation:

8 Time and Place
Listening to make inferences

Directions: Today we have a short story about a boy named Cisco. As you listen to the story, try to find out if the time is day or night and if the season is winter or summer.

The clock on the town hall struck four. Cisco tugged at his jacket and zipped up the front. The wind was getting colder.

"This business of carrying the last lawn chairs into the basement is pretty hard work," Cisco thought to himself. "I should have finished up this job six weeks ago."

Just then the side door opened and Mrs. Walters came out. "Cisco, finish your work as quickly as you can. It's getting dark already, and it's supposed to snow tonight."

Discussion:
Evaluation:

9 Private Eye
Listening to make inferences

Directions: Listen carefully to this short article about the moon. As I read, listen for clues why none of the plants and animals on earth could live on the moon without special protection.

If you look up in the sky, the moon looks flat, but we know that the moon is a sphere just as the earth is. United States astronauts have orbited the moon and landed on the moon's surface. Now we know much more about the moon than people did even ten years ago.

Long ago, people made up stories saying that the moon was made of green cheese, or that it was a flat circle set up in the sky, or even that the moon was the sun's wife. Long ago, people laughed and said that there was a man in the moon. We know now that mountains, craters, and rocks make it look as if there were a face visible to us on earth.

The astronauts found no water on the moon. They bring air and food supplies with them in the rocket. On the moon, days and nights are two weeks long. The days are hot enough to make water boil, and the nights are far colder than our nights on earth.

Discussion:
Evaluation:

10 What Happens Next?
Listening to predict outcomes

Directions: Today we have a story about two children and their mother. As you will hear, they are all on a sight-seeing trip in New

York. Listen carefully, for these three people are going to have some interesting experiences. Just as the story gets interesting, you will have to supply the ending in your own way.

It was their first visit to New York and, certainly, it was their first visit to one of the biggest department stores in the world. Mrs. Davis and her two children, Nanette and Kenny, were rushed into the revolving doors by the breathless Christmas shoppers.

Inside the department store, holiday decorations glittered, and Nanette and Kenny thought that they had never seen so many people. They made their way to the elevators and looked at the long store directory on the wall.

"What shall we do first?" asked Mrs. Davis.

"Toys! Let's go to the toy department," exclaimed Nanette, and Kenny nodded his head happily.

"Well, I have to look for some shoes," said Mrs. Davis. "I saw a sign back there saying there was a sale on walking shoes, and my feet really need something comfortable. You two go on to the toy department and look around. In half an hour, come to meet me in the shoe department."

Kenny and Nanette rode up in the elevator to the eighth floor and the toy department. What fun it was to see the games of all kinds, dolls, and stuffed animals of all sizes, wind-up toys, and books. Suddenly, Nanette looked at the clock. "Wow! It's time to go find Mom."

"Let's go find another store directory by the elevators so we can find the shoe department. The children looked under "S" in the long directory on the wall. Kenny read aloud, "Shoes, Women's—second floor, fourth floor, fifth floor, and seventh floor."

Then Nanette said softly, "How will we find her?"

Discussion:
Evaluation:

Part 2

Listening Games for the Primary Grades

There are two major purposes for giving children in the primary grades directed learning experiences. First, they learn how to listen for specific purposes, and second, they learn how to respond verbally. In addition to the give and take of discussion sessions like those in Part *1*, there may be times when the teacher will want to create a game-like atmosphere with the aid of simple response cards. These are particularly suited to the primary grades. Listening selections used with the game approach need to be literal enough to allow the children to indicate their answers with an arrow, a card, or a number of discs.

The best game situations occur in small groups when the teacher, an aide, or an older student helps to maintain the suspense and secrecy of the game. First you read the selection, then there is a short period of silence while each child decides on his answer and manipulates his response card to show it. Afterward, be sure to encourage the children's verbal responses. In the event that disagreements arise, you should read the selection again. In fact, you may have to read it several times until the children catch on. Problems such as this one are among the items you'll want to note in your anecdotal evaluation of each listening experience.

Although the discussion period following each game is valuable, it is not vital. There may be times you will want to use listening experiences as purely diagnostic tools, either for the class as a whole, or for small groups working in a learning center. In both cases you will need to provide students with the appropriate response materials—work boards, crayons, pencils, cards, or markers. Directions for making several response cards are included in this part.

The games in Part 2 are based on the children's knowledge of colors and color names, numerals and selected math processes, basic reading readiness skills, and directions such as *left* or *bottom*. As a diagnostic tool, these games can also reveal the need for teaching or reteaching some of these basic concepts. The titles of these games give away the answers, so do not read them to the students.

Some cautions regarding the use of manipulative devices should be mentioned here. Might one of the boys be color blind? Would muscular coordination play a role in some children's ability to turn an arrow, draw a straight line, or put a small card into an individual pocket? Do some children have hearing or visual handicaps? How can you organize the games to be so interesting that even the most volatile children want to participate—and cooperate? What can you do to encourage the shy child who is so afraid of getting the wrong answer? Your anecdotal evaluations from Part *1* will be of invaluable assistance in planning for these games.

COLOR GAMES

USING THE COLOR WHEEL

The games in this section are based on the assumption that the children can identify selected colors. If they cannot, then adaptations can be made. This wheel device can also be used to teach color names by having the children match, say, an orange marker to the orange section of the color wheel by both color and color name. For the younger children, it is best to begin with only four colors instead of eight. The sections may also be labeled with color names, if color word recognition is one of your aims.

CONSTRUCTING THE COLOR WHEEL

Using oaktag or cardboard, cut one circle 6″ in diameter for each child who will play the game. Divide the circle into eight (or four) sections as shown below. Cut eight sections, this size, out of eight different sheets of colored construction paper. Paste them in place on the color wheel. Cut a 6″ circle from colorless adhesive paper and smooth it over the construction paper; this will help preserve the color wheels for many uses. From oaktag, cut an arrow 2½″ long and attach it to the center of the circle with a paper fastener.

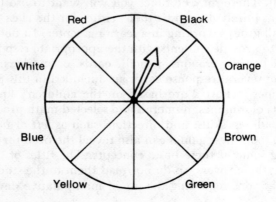

1 *The Green Mittens*
Listening for details

Directions: Today we'll hear a short story about a girl named Lisa who lost her new mittens. Keep your color wheels in your hands because I'm going to ask you to listen carefully to find out what color Lisa's mittens were. When the story is over, you can show me the color of Lisa's mittens by turning the arrow on your color wheel to that color.

Lisa lost her new mittens at school. Her teacher asked her to describe the mittens to the rest of the boys and girls in the class. This is what Lisa said:

"I lost my new mittens yesterday. I think I left them on the playground after morning recess. My aunt made them for me and gave them to me for my birthday. The mittens are green, and they're a little bit big for me because my aunt said I'd probably grow a lot this year. If you find them, let me know."

With your color wheel, pick out the color. In a few moments, we'll all show the color and talk about the story. . . . Now, hold up your color wheels.

Discussion:
Evaluation:

2 *The Orange Frosting*
Listening for details

Directions: Here is a story about two children, John and Sherry, who decorated some cookies for a special party. Keep your color wheels close beside you because you'll use them to answer a question about the story. Listen carefully so you can find out the color of the frosting that John used to cover the big, round cookies.

John and his sister were making Halloween cookies. The round cookies were baked and cooled so they could be decorated. John had mixed some sugar frosting to cover the top of each cooky. He wanted to make the round cookies look like pumpkins, so he mixed orange food coloring into his frosting. Working carefully, John spread some orange frosting over the top of each cooky.

Sherry was mixing some chocolate frosting in a small bowl. When John's orange frosting was dry on each cooky, Sherry added two brown dots for eyes, one brown dot for a nose, and a smiling brown mouth on each one.

When the cookies were decorated, John and Sherry decided that these were the best Halloween jack o'lantern cookies they had ever seen.

Now use the arrow on your color wheel to point to the color that John used for the frosting on top of every cooky. . . . Now, hold up your color wheels.

Discussion:
Evaluation:

3   *The Yellow Kite*
Listening for details

Directions: Listen carefully while I read a story to you about a girl named Vicky. Keep your color wheel close by because you'll need it to answer a question about the story. Vicky wants to buy a kite, and as you hear the story, listen to find out exactly what color the kite was that Vicky bought.

It was a windy March day, and Vicky was very excited about buying a new kite. She had saved her money, and now she was standing in the game and hobby shop looking over the kites. She had been in the shop many times, and she thought she knew which kite she wanted. That big red box kite was great, but it cost too much money. There were two other kites, one green and one red, but they looked too hard for her to put together without a lot of help. Vicky had seen a yellow kite that looked fairly easy to put together. She looked at this kite again. She had saved enough money to buy this kite, so she bought the last one she saw. Vicky knew this one would be a good flying kite.

Use your color wheel now. Turn the arrow to the color of the kite that Vicky bought. When you have all picked out the color, we'll hold up our color wheels. . . . Now, show me what color it was.

Discussion:
Evaluation:

4 *The Blue Sneakers*
Listening for details

Directions: Here's a story about Leo who was going to buy a new pair of shoes. He wasn't very happy about going into the shoe store, but, as you will see, he found a pair of shoes he liked. Keep your color wheel handy because I'm going to ask you to use it when I finish reading the story. Listen carefully to find out what color the shoes were that Leo bought.

"Going shopping is bad enough," thought Leo, "but trying on shoes is the worst thing yet!" Leo and his mother were sitting in the shoe store, and the salesman had just measured Leo's feet.

"It's almost summer," said Leo's mother. "You need a pair of shoes that are light and comfortable. How about some sneakers?"

"How about that!" said Leo. "Good idea, but what color can I pick?"

"Any color you want," answered his mother. "All of these new shoes can be washed and dried, and they'll be as good as new."

Leo was feeling much better when the salesman brought out three boxes of shoes in Leo's size. First, Leo tried on black sneakers, but they looked too much like his winter shoes. Then the salesman had Leo try on some blue sneakers. Leo asked the man what color shoes were in the last box. These were white sneakers.

"Those white shoes would be dirty all the time," Leo said looking at his mother. "I think I'd like to have the second pair of shoes I tried on. How about it, Mom?"

With your color wheel, turn the arrow to the color of the shoes Leo liked best. These were the second pair of shoes he tried on. . . . Now, hold up your color wheels.

Discussion:
Evaluation:

5 *The Brown Bird*
Listening to make inferences

Directions: Listen carefully to this winter story about a girl named May Ann and a little bird. As you hear this story, listen carefully to see if you can find out what color the little winter bird was. When

I'm finished reading the story, you can use your color wheel to show the color of the bird.

May Ann walked for three blocks along the snowy street one afternoon on her way home from school. The white snow crunched under her feet, and the wind whirled the powdery snow all around. She pulled her red knitted hat down over her ears a little more tightly. Suddenly, she heard a bird singing. The sound on such a still, snowy afternoon made her stop and look all around.

Again, the bird's cheery song could be heard. It seemed to come from one direction, but there was only an old, brown oak tree where May Ann looked. The old tree had no leaves since winter had come. As May Ann stared at the tree, she heard the chirping sound again. Looking at all of the bare branches, May Ann noticed a tiny bird moving about. That was the bird all right! No wonder it was so hard to see the bird. He was about the same color as the old tree.

With your color wheel, turn the arrow to the color that matches the little bird. Think for a minute, then we'll all show the color and talk about the story. . . . Now, hold up your color wheels.

Discussion:
Evaluation:

6 The Red Riddle
Listening to make inferences

Directions: Now we have a color riddle. Pick up your color wheel because you will need to look at it as I read the riddle. Listen carefully as I read, and look at your color wheel, for you need to do a lot of remembering in this riddle. When I finish reading, we'll use our color wheels to find out who has been able to guess the color.

I am not green like the grass, and I am not orange like the round, juicy fruit we eat. I am not blue, either. My name isn't yellow, and it isn't black. I am not brown, and I'm not white. Please help me. What color am I?

Turn the arrow on your color wheel to the color that this riddle is talking about. Take a little time to think of all the colors that were mentioned in the riddle and see if you can help this one color that has lost his name. . . . Now, hold up your color wheels.

Discussion:
Evaluation:

MATH GAMES

USING THE INDIVIDUAL CARD HOLDER

In math work with children at the primary level, individual card holders can be used to facilitate learning while practicing math concepts. Story problems lend themselves well to use as listening experiences. Students show their answers by using an accompanying pack of numeral cards or cards bearing dots or symbols. The first listening experiences in this part call for the use of symbol cards, and the remainder require numeral cards.

CONSTRUCTING THE INDIVIDUAL CARD HOLDER

Make one individual card holder for each child. Oaktag is best for this purpose. Cut the card holders 9" X 5", then fold up the bottom 1½" along the length and staple it in front to form a shallow pocket. Cut several 4" X 3" response cards for each player and label them with the numerals and dots they'll need to answer the problems. To show his answer, the student selects the appropriate game card, places it in the pocket on the card holder, and holds it up for you to see.

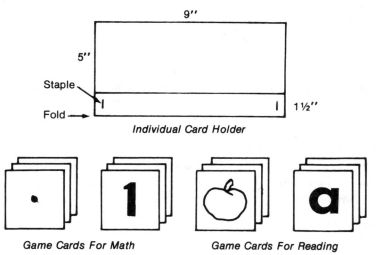

Individual Card Holder

Game Cards For Math   *Game Cards For Reading*

7   *Five Birds*
Listening for specific details

Directions: Today, we are going to hear a story about some birds. Keep your dot cards close by because I want to see if you can listen carefully and tell me how many birds there were in all. When the story is finished, you pick out the dot card that tells the number of birds the children saw.

Four birds were eating at the feeding station outside of the first grade classroom windows. As the children watched the birds, one more bird fluttered down to join the others.

Now, pick out the dot card that shows the number of birds the children saw. Think for a minute, and then we'll look at each other's cards. . . . Ready? Hold up your dot cards.

Discussion:
Evaluation:

8   *Seven Comic Books*
Listening for specific details

Directions: Here is a story about Randy, a boy who decided to pick up his room. Right now he is picking up some comic books. Listen to see how many comic books he finds. When the story is over, you pick out the dot card that tells the number of comic books he finds.

Randy was trying to clean up his room. He decided to put his comic books in one pile. He found two comic books on the top of his bookshelf. After looking carefully in his closet, he found five more comic books there. He put all of them in one pile. How many comic books did Randy find?

Find the dot card that tells the number and put it in your card holder. Then, after we show our cards, we'll talk about the story. . . . Now, hold up your dot cards.

Discussion:
Evaluation:

9 Two Apples
Listening for specific details

Directions: Here's a story about Anita who is going to use some apples to make dessert. Hold on to your dot cards because you will be using one of them to answer a question. Here is the question: How many apples are going to be left in the bowl after Anita cooks the ones she needs? Listen carefully.

> Anita decided to make baked apples for dessert. She knew she had six apples in the bowl. Anita took four apples and fixed them for baking. She only needed to bake four apples.

Think about how many apples were left in the bowl. When you have your answer, put your dot card into your card holder. . . . Ready? Hold up your dot cards.

Discussion:
Evaluation:

10 Five Easels
Listening for specific details

Directions: All boys and girls like to paint, and painting on easels makes it even more fun. Listen carefully to this story of a second grade classroom that had eight easels. One day some easels were borrowed. Try to find out how many easels were left in the second grade classroom after that. Keep your dot cards handy to answer this question.

> The second grade classroom had eight easels that the children used for painting. One day, the first grade teacher asked if she could borrow three of the easels for the day. She promised to return them the very next day. How many of the eight easels were left in the second grade classroom?

Think carefully, then pick out the dot card that tells how many easels were left. Put the dot card in your holder. . . . Now, hold up your cards.

Discussion:
Evaluation:

11   Eight Blocks
Listening for specific details

Directions: Here is a story that tells about Jeff and his long walk. Listen carefully, for I want you to tell me how many blocks Jeff walks. Keep your numeral cards handy. When I finish reading, I'll give you some time to put the numeral card in the card holder.

Jeff decided to count how many blocks he had to walk from his house to his friend's house. Barry was his friend, and Jeff liked to visit him. But it seemed like such a long way to Barry's house.

Jeff walked for three blocks along his own street. Then he turned right at the drugstore on the corner and walked for five more blocks before he reached Barry's house. How many blocks did Jeff walk altogether?

Think carefully, then pick out the numeral card that you think tells the answer. Put your card in the holder. . . . Now, show me your answer.

Discussion:
Evaluation:

12   Ten Cans
Listening for specific details

Directions: Today we have the story of Mrs. Gomez who has just gone shopping for food. See if you can tell how many cans of food Mrs. Gomez bought. After the story, you can show me the numeral card that tells the answer.

Mrs. Gomez was putting away the cans of food that she had just bought at the supermarket. As she put away the cans in a cupboard, she decided to count how many cans she had bought. First, she put away three cans of soup. Then she put three cans of green beans in front of the soup. Two cans of corn went into the cupboard next, and finally, Mrs. Gomez put away two cans of peaches.

"I've done quite a bit of shopping today," thought Mrs. Gomez.

How many cans of food did Mrs. Gomez buy? Choose the card

that you think tells the number of cans. Place your card in the holder. . . . Now, show your answer.

Discussion:
Evaluation:

13 Three Cookies
Listening for specific details

Directions: Chris liked cookies, but one day he had a problem about how many he should eat. Listen to the story about Chris and see if you can answer his question.

When Chris got home from school, he found a note on the kitchen table. The note read:

Chris,
I'll be home a little later. Drink a glass of milk, and eat half the cookies on the plate. Save the other half for Don who will be home about four o'clock.

Mom

Chris counted the cookies on the plate. There were six chocolate chip cookies. He thought, "How many can I eat so that Don can have the same number when he gets home?"

How many cookies could Chris eat? Think about the problem, then put the numeral card that answers the question in your card holder. . . . Now, hold up your answers.

Discussion:
Evaluation:

14 Eight Invitations
Listening for specific details

Directions: Have you ever made invitations for a party? Listen to this story about a group of children who were making invitations at school. They finished some invitations, and they wanted to find out how many more invitations they had to make. Listen to the story and see if you can answer the question.

Some of the children in Room 24 were working as a committee to make invitations for their Thanksgiving play. They were inviting the other third grade rooms, the school nurse, the librarian, the principal, and some other special guests. Altogether, they needed to make fifteen invitations. They counted the invitations that were finished and put them in one pile. There were seven. How many more invitations would the committee have to make so that they would have fifteen?

Think carefully. When you think you know, place the numeral card that answers the question in your card holder. . . . All right, show me your answers.

Discussion:
Evaluation:

READING GAMES

USING PICTURE CARDS

To augment the program of reading instruction in the initial stages, certain phases of reading readiness and beginning reading can be utilized as listening games. Maintaining the game atmosphere is important in this area as well as in math. For the next few listening activities, you'll need to make ten cards with the following pictures for each player. The following list is only an example. You'll want to include pictures that meet the needs of your children. (Do not number the cards.)

Card 1	shoes	Card 6	table
Card 2	bicycle	Card 7	wagon
Card 3	apple	Card 8	glass
Card 4	baseball bat	Card 9	turtle
Card 5	window	Card 10	gloves

Using your picture cards, you can design listening games to practice: (1) using context clues to complete a single-sentence story, (2) detecting words that begin with the same sounds, (3) and with some modifications or additions to the cards, affixing the lower case beginning letter(s) to a picture to indicate a knowledge of sound-symbol relationships.

15 *Story Sentences*
Listening to make inferences

Directions: Today, you each have a pack of ten picture cards to use with your card holders. Spread the cards out on the table in front of you in any order you wish. Take a good look at all of them. I'll read a short story sentence to you, and I'll leave out the last word. One of the pictures will fit the sentence very well. Listen carefully as I read the first sentence. Pick out the picture and put it in your card holder, then we'll show our pictures and talk about the sentence.

(Read the sentences one at a time, allowing adequate time for picture selection and discussion after each one. The following examples illustrate the type of sentence stories you might use. Allow adequate time for discussion after each activity.)

1. Jerry put his feet into his new _____.
2. Michelle liked to ride on her two-wheeled _____.
3. In her lunch box, Linda had an _____.
4. To play baseball, you need to have a ball and a _____.
5. Joe saw that it was raining when he looked out the _____.
6. Mother called, "Your dinner is ready and on the _____.
7. Janet's little sister pulled her dog in her little _____.
8. Toby poured some milk into a _____.
9. "Mr. Slow" was the name of Herb's new pet _____.
10. Nancy's hands were cold because she had lost her _____.

Discussion:
Evaluation:

16 *Beginning Sounds*
Listening for beginning sounds

For this listening activity, you might try grouping the picture cards into two packets by beginning sounds, then have the children work with one packet at a time:

Packet 1		Packet 2	
Card 2	bicycle	Card 5	window
Card 4	bat	Card 7	wagon
Card 6	table	Card 8	glass
Card 9	turtle	Card 10	gloves
Card 1	shoes	Card 3	apple

Directions: Spread out your packet of five cards and look at all of the pictures. Say the names of the things on your picture cards to yourself. Now, I'm going to say three words to you that all begin with the same sound. After I say these three words to you, pick out any of your picture cards which begin with the same sound. If one or even two pictures do begin with the same sound, place that picture or pictures in the card holder.

Here are the first three words. Listen carefully.

glitter	gleam	glad

Are there any pictures on your cards of things which begin with the same sound as glitter, gleam, and glad? If so, put them in your card holder. . . . Show them to me now.

(Allow adequate time for discussion after each activity.)

Here are some other word combinations you might try:

toes	tip	tent
shirt	shut	shell
boat	bean	butter
worm	wish	watch
ant	address	after
laugh	ladder	leap

Discussion:
Evaluation:

17   *Beginning Letters*
Listening for beginning sounds

For this listening activity, you'll need to make two more sets of cards for use with Packets 1 and 2:

for Packet 1		for Packet 2	
Card 1	*b*	Card 1	*w*
Card 2	*t*	Card 2	*g*
Card 3	*sh*	Card 3	*a*
Card 4	*r*	Card 4	*p*

Directions: Today, you have two packets of cards—picture cards and letter cards. I'm going to ask you to follow some new directions for this game. Spread out your picture cards on one side of the table, and spread out your letter cards on the other side. Now, listen carefully.

1. Pick up the pictures of the bat and the bicycle and put them into your card holder. Now put down your card holder and look for the card that shows the letter or letters that begin the words *bat* and *bicycle*.

As soon as you find that letter card, put it in your card holder. . . . Ready? Hold up your cards. (Allow adequate time for discussion after each activity.)

The following pictures and letters can be used to complete the work of Packet 1; use the same procedure for Packet 2.

2. table	turtle	*t*
3. shoes	—	*sh*
4. —	—	*r*

Discussion:
Evaluation:

FOLLOWING DIRECTIONS

USING THE INDIVIDUAL CHALKBOARD/FELTBOARD

The use of small, individual chalkboards and feltboards in conjunction with listening activities can help primary level children learn to follow directions and develop a feel for sequence. Games which help them practice directions (top, bottom, left, right) and attend to aspects of sequence are suggested in this section. Each player will need pieces of chalk and/or felt geometric shapes. Some of the games will require that quadrants be marked on the boards.

CONSTRUCTING THE INDIVIDUAL CHALKBOARD/ FELTBOARD

Individual chalkboards can be purchased commercially. By glueing a piece of felt on the back, you can have a handy two-in-one board for each child.

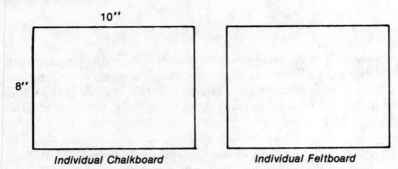

Individual Chalkboard   *Individual Feltboard*

You can also make individual feltboards using shoe boxes and cigar boxes. The boxes serve as storage places for the felt geometric shapes, while the inside of the box tops, covered with felt, become the feltboards.

Cut the following felt geometric shapes for each child:

Circles	Squares	Equilateral Triangles
(1½″ diameter)	(1½″ × 1½″)	(1½″ base)
3 red	3 red	3 red
3 blue	3 blue	3 blue
3 green	3 green	3 green

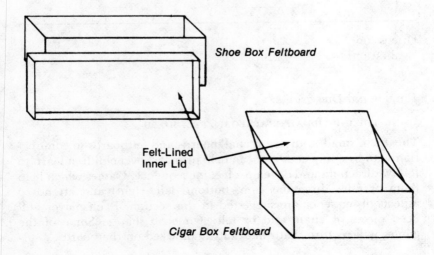

Shoe Box Feltboard

Felt-Lined
Inner Lid

Cigar Box Feltboard

18 X's and O's
Listening to follow instructions

Directions: (You'll need to mark quadrants on the chalkboards for these activities.) Today we're going to play some games using your chalkboards and chalk. I'm going to read one sentence and you will mark on your chalkboard what I ask. Your chalkboard is divided into four parts to help you. After every sentence, we'll stop and show our answers, then talk about them.

1. Mark an X in the top right side of your chalkboard. Think about it, then put your X on the top right side. . . . Now, show me your chalkboards.

2. Mark an X in the bottom left side of your chalkboard.

3. Mark an O in the bottom right side of your chalkboard.

4. Mark an O in the top left side of your chalkboard.

5. Now let's pretend your chalkboard is a playground divided into four parts. Two X's are playing in the bottom right side of the playground. Use your chalk to mark where the two X's are playing.

6. Two O's are playing ball on the bottom left side of the playground. Show on your chalkboard where these two O's are playing.

7. Three X's are jumping rope in the top right side of the playground. Mark these three X's in their place on the playground.

8. Two O's are playing tether ball in the top right side of the playground. With your chalk, mark where the two O's are standing.

9. The teacher is standing right in the middle of the playground. With an X, mark that spot.

Discussion:
Evaluation:

19 Lines in All Directions
Listening to follow instructions

Directions: Today, we'll play another chalkboard game to find out just what good listeners you are. I'll read you a sentence that will tell you exactly what to do with your chalk. Listen carefully. (Allow adequate time for discussion after each activity.)

1. Draw a line from the top left corner of your chalkboard all the way across to the bottom right corner. Listen again. Draw a line from the top left corner to the bottom right corner. . . . Ready? Hold up your chalkboards.

2. Starting any place you want at the top of your chalkboard, draw a line straight down to the bottom of your chalkboard. (Comments and close attention to the children's work will aid you in evaluating their progress. You might say, "Good! Now show me where you started your lines.")

3. Draw a line from the bottom left corner of your chalkboard all the way across to the top right corner of your chalkboard. (Say: "Point to where you started your line.")

4. Starting any place you want at the bottom of your chalkboard, draw a line straight up to the top of your chalkboard. (Say: "Point to where you started your line.")

5. Listen carefully, for I am going to ask you to follow two directions. Make a capital *A* on the right side of your chalkboard. Now, make a capital *B* on the left side of your chalkboard.

6. Here are three directions for you to follow: Put an *A* on the right side of your chalkboard, a *C* on the left side of your chalkboard, and a *B* between the *A* and the *C*.

Discussion:
Evaluation:

20 *Designs in Red*
Listening to remember sequence

Directions: (Use only red geometric shapes for this activity.)

Today we will work with red circles, squares, and triangles on our feltboards. We'll make different kinds of designs with them. You'll need to listen carefully. For instance, I might say: (Demonstrate) Start at the left and work toward the right. First put down one circle. Now put one square right beside it. Put down a triangle last.

After we make a design, we'll look at them and talk about the design.

1. Working from left to right, put down a circle and then, beside it, put down a square. Ready? . . . Let's check them.

2. Working from left to right, put down a triangle, then a circle, then another triangle.

3. Working from left to right, put down one circle, then put two squares beside it.

4. Working from left to right, put down one square, then one triangle, then one circle.

5. Working from left to right, put down two triangles first, and then two squares.

Using the blue and the green sets of felt shapes, give the children additional practice in listening to follow directions and to follow sequence. Other games can be developed by building designs from the bottom to the top, or the top to the bottom of the feltboard.

Discussion:
Evaluation:

21 The Necklace
Listening to remember sequence

Directions: Today our listening games will be harder and more fun. Pay close attention. Organize all of the triangles, circles, and squares by color. All of your circles should be in one spot, with the red circles in one pile, the blue circles in another pile, and the green ones in one pile. Organize your triangles the same way—red triangles in one pile, blue triangles in one pile, and green triangles in one pile. Work on your squares, too.

We're going to make some colorful designs today. Listen carefully to each story so that you can make the design yourself. We'll all compare designs when you're finished. After each design, we'll talk about the story.

1. Jan decided she wanted to make a pretty necklace by stringing some round, painted beads she had at home. She decided to try out her design first by using the feltboard and the circles she had at school.

First, Jan put a red circle at the very left side of her felt-board. After the red circle, she put down a blue circle, and then she put down a green circle. So Jan had a red circle, a blue circle, and then a green circle. She decided to follow the same plan, so she continued the design by adding three more circles—first, another red circle, then another blue circle, and last, another green circle. Jan looked at her six-circle design to see if she liked it.

Now, you see if you can make the design that Jan made. We'll wait until everyone is ready, and then we'll compare our designs. Perhaps we'll have to listen to the story again. . . . Now, hold up your feltboards.

2. Jan decided to try another design for her necklace. She used her feltboard and the circles again. This time, Jan started at the left side of her feltboard with two red circles. Then she added a green one. Let's see, she had two red circles and one green circle. After this, she added two blue circles and a green circle. Her design looked like this: two red circles and one green, then two blue circles and one green. Jan looked at her six-circle design to see if she liked it.

Now, you see if you can make the design Jan made this time. When everyone is ready, we'll look at our designs. We can always listen to the story again. . . . Ready with your designs?

Discussion:
Evaluation:

22 A Geometric Monster
Listening to remember sequence

Directions: Here is a story about Charlie, who decided to use his feltboard and colored shapes to make a monster from outer space. Listen carefully and see if you can make the same kind of monster Charlie made.

Charlie decided that his monster should have a blue triangle sit-ting right on top of a blue square body. Because his monster had wheels instead of feet, Charlie put two red circles below the blue body. For arms, the monster had two red triangles coming out of the two sides of his blue body. What a monster!

Now, can you make a monster that looks like Charlie's? Try to remember how his monster was made. When you're ready, we'll listen to the story again, and you can check your monster against Charlie's. . . . Finish your monsters.

Discussion:
Evaluation:

23 Funny Cars
Listening to remember sequence

Directions: Today, we have a story about Barbara who uses her feltboard and colored shapes to design a funny car. Listen carefully so you can make a car like Barbara did with your felt shapes.

Barbara decided to try to make a funny car on her feltboard. First, she put down two red squares for the body of the car. Then she decided to try two blue circles for the wheels. On the right side of the car, Barbara put a green triangle. This was to be the front of the car. Barbara needed a top on her car, so she put a green square on top of the two blue squares.

Now, you try to make a car that looks like Barbara's. Work on it for a while, then we'll listen to the story again and compare our funny cars. . . . Ready? Hold up your feltboards.

Discussion:
Evaluation:

Part 3
Evaluating Advertisements

TO THE TEACHER

Advertising is firmly entrenched as part of modern life, and it's not likely to disappear soon. Children hear radio and television commercials before they can read. Billboards and newspaper and magazine ads are with us in profusion. Advertisements give us a variety of information about new products, techniques, services, and prices. Advertising campaigns range from multi-million dollar Madison Avenue efforts, to the hastily written notices on supermarket bulletin boards.

Today, television is the major source of advertising that children are exposed to. Mass market television advertising is designed to meet or create our needs, desires, and even, some say, our values. The children's television series "Sesame Street" has utilized the repetitive aspects of the conventional TV commercial by repeating several segments involving specific letters and numerals throughout each program and by announcing, at the conclusion of each program, that the program was "brought to you by the letters *b* and *r* and the number 7," or whatever letters and numerals were featured during that particular program.

There are indications that children, as well as adults, are becoming increasingly sophisticated in evaluating some of the superlatives and claims made in advertisements. The listening activities in this section will help them sharpen these skills. It won't be long before you have some lively discussions concerning apparent honesty in ads, ads that seem to help people, and advertising gimmicks.

The listening activities in Part 3 are organized in the following manner:

1- 6 Public Service Ads

7-11 Miscellaneous Ads

12-14 Straight Ads

15-26 Exaggerated Ads

The public service ads deal with no particular product but instead provide straight information concerning family life, health and environmental measures, and community and general interest announcements. The second group of listening experiences is found frequently in the classified sections of newspapers under the heading "Miscellaneous," or on supermarket bulletin boards. The commercial ads in the last two sections mirror some of the techniques of contemporary advertising geared to the consumer and relying on snob or reverse snob appeal, the folksy "down home" touch, the heartfelt testimonial, or the honest-to-goodness sale announcement.

The listening activities are arranged in this order only for the convenience of the teacher. Present them in any order you like. Consider your students and their background in evaluative thinking, and start from there. Build your own collection of ads from all media, and ask the children to contribute, too. Then, as you begin to work through the various kinds of ads, commercials, and announcements, the types and classifications will become apparent. The precise terminology for these is not important. Instead, you will want to emphasize the information ads contain and how the children as consumers can evaluate this information.

Simply stated, the study of advertising will lead the elementary child into the following basic analysis:

1. Who is presenting the information?

2. For what purpose is the information transmitted?

3. What are the responsibilities of the receiver?

1 *Public Service Ad*
Listening to evaluate advertising

Directions: It was almost time for Roy's favorite TV program, so he turned on the TV set and sat down on the floor to watch. Before the show started, Roy heard a commercial that told the audience how to take care of their teeth. In a moment you'll hear the same commercial Roy did. As you listen to it, first ask yourself why you think the commercial was being broadcast. Second, have you heard any other commercials about taking care of your teeth? Were the other commercials different from this one? Listen carefully. Here is the commercial:

We all need to take care of our teeth. Here are some helpful hints that will help you take care of your teeth:

1. Go easy on between-meal snacks, especially sweets. Raisins, oranges, apples, and carrot and celery sticks make good snacks.

2. Brush your teeth after every meal. If you can't brush, rinse out your mouth with water several times, or eat an apple. Apples are sometimes called "nature's toothbrushes."

3. See your dentist regularly for check-ups.

Now, let's go over the questions.

Discussion:
Evaluation:

• 2 *Public Service Ad*
Listening to evaluate advertising

Directions: One day, Pauline brought home a letter from school about the Spring Carnival. She was very excited as she read it to her mother and her older brother. The letter she read was an announcement. We'll hear the letter that Pauline read. While you are listening, decide if this announcement is a good one. Does it give all the information that Pauline and her family need to know? Listen carefully to see what you can find out about the time, the place, and the cost of the school carnival.

Dear Parents and Children of W.R. Miller School,
On Saturday, May 15, our school will hold a Spring Carnival on

the school grounds from two o'clock in the afternoon until 7:30 at night. This is our regular celebration for the children, teachers, parents, and friends of Miller School.

There will be booths with special games, a merry-go-round, and a Ferris wheel ride. Each game and ride will cost 10¢. Cartoons will be shown for 10¢ in the all-purpose room from 3 p.m. to 4 p.m. At four o'clock, the boys and girls of the fifth and sixth grades will challenge the teachers to a game of baseball. Then at 5:30 p.m. an Italian dinner will be served in the cafeteria. The cost of the dinner will be $1.50 for adults and $.70 for children.

We hope you can come with the whole family for a part of the day, or stay all afternoon and evening on Saturday, May 15.

Sincerely,

Elizabeth R. Bowen
Principal

That's the letter Pauline read. Did it give you enough information about the Spring Carnival? What information can you remember? (During the discussion, you might want to bring out the point that a printed message can always be reread, while the listener can only depend on his or her memory.)

Discussion:
Evaluation:

3 Public Service Ad
Listening to evaluate advertising

Directions: Chuck was listening to the radio when he heard the announcer start to talk about safety at home. Chuck decided to listen carefully to find out why the announcer was talking about safety. You listen to find out if the announcer is trying to get his listeners to buy any particular kind of product. Here is the commercial:

Now that spring is here, it's time to clean up, paint up, and fix up inside and outside of the house. Before you start your outside work, here are a few tips. Are you planning to trim some tall bushes? How about cleaning the outside of some high windows? Will you paint the outside of your house? Our station suggests that one of the first things you should check is your stepladder. Make sure that it is firm and steady. Check each step to be sure it will hold your weight. Check to see that metal parts are strong and that the bolts have not rusted. Our station wants you to stay well and healthy. Take your transistor radio outside and, while you work, listen to our latest news and weather reports, and our special music.

Why do you think the announcer was talking about safety?

Discussion:
Evaluation:

4 *Public Service Ad*
Listening to evaluate advertising

Directions: Patrolman Ralph Martinez was talking to the children of Room 19. He was giving them some advice and information. You can listen to the last part of his talk. Do you think the speaker knows his subject and is qualified to talk about this topic? Here is the way Patrolman Martinez ended his talk. You listen, too.

When you're walking home from school, be very sure to look both ways when you cross a street that has no traffic lights. If you have to cross a street that does have a traffic light, first look to see if there is a "walk" button to push. The "walk" light tells you exactly when you may cross the street. If there is no "walk" button, wait until you see the green light, then cross the street. Always cross at a corner and walk in the pedestrian crossing. If you follow these simple rules, you'll be home safely in no time.

The next time I visit your room, we'll talk about bicycle safety. Right now, accident prevention is up to you. You can do a great deal to help teach your younger brothers and sisters and neighbors about safe ways to cross streets.

Do you think Patrolman Martinez was qualified to talk about accident prevention? Do you suppose he has had some experience with traffic safety and with traffic accidents?

Discussion:
Evaluation:

5 *Public Service Ad*
Listening to evaluate advertising

Directions: It was Friday, the thirteenth, and Pete was watching a special television show about superstitions called "Bad Luck Day." The master of ceremonies was talking with some people about old superstitions—where they came from, and whether they were really true. Everyone had agreed that these old sayings were not true. You listen along with Pete to the concluding statements of the master of ceremonies. As you listen, ask yourself if the man is trying to sell a particular product to you. Ask yourself if he is trying to make you think in a particular way. Here is the conclusion of the program:

So, my friends, as you walk out on the street today and start toward home, don't be worried if a black cat runs in front of you. No one believes that cats have any magic properties at all. That cat is probably in a hurry to get home, too. And as you walk down the street, forget the old rhyme, "If you step on a crack, you break your mother's back." It's just not so! You might want to walk around a painter's ladder instead of under it—not because it's bad luck to walk under a ladder, but just to avoid getting paint splatters on your clothes.

Friday the thirteenth is not a bad luck day. It's just another day when you think of all the superstitions that people used to worry about long ago. Oh, yes! And if you happen to break a mirror when you get home, don't worry about having seven years of bad luck, because that's not true, either. If you break a mirror, all you have to worry about is picking up the pieces without cutting yourself, then start planning to save some money for a new one.

Was the master of ceremonies trying to sell a particular product? What do you suppose his message to his viewers really was?

Discussion:
Evaluation:

6   *Public Service Ad*
Listening to evaluate advertising

Directions: Jennifer was listening to his radio one Friday afternoon when, suddenly, a voice said, "Here is a special message presented in the community interest." Jennifer decided to listen carefully to see if she could determine if this was really going to be a special message, or if the announcer was just going to give a regular commercial. You listen along with Jennifer to help her determine what kind of a message the announcer read.

Tomorrow, a free Polio Clinic will be held at River Bend High School. If you have never received the vaccine before, this is the time to protect yourself against this crippling disease. People who have not had a booster in the five years since their first vaccine are urged to come to the clinic. People of all ages need protection from polio. Parents are asked to accompany children under 18 years of age.

How would you describe the message that the announcer gave?

Discussion:
Evaluation:

7 *Miscellaneous Ad*
Listening to evaluate advertising

Directions: Glen and his friend Russ went to the supermarket to buy some food for a camping trip. As they walked through the door into the market, they stopped by the Community Bulletin Board where people post signs and notices. Glen said, "Hey, Russ! Here's an interesting notice. Listen to this." Then Glen read that one particularly interesting notice to Russ.

You listen to the notice and try to decide what the writer wants to do.

Want to Trade Comic Books?

I have a large collection of old, old comic books — and some new ones, too. I would be willing to trade some treasures with anyone else who has a comic book collection. I really want old copies of *Batman, Superman,* and *Captain Marvel* magazines.

Call Willie R.
271-5613 after 5 p.m.

What do you think was the reason for this notice? What do you think the writer of this ad wanted to accomplish?

Discussion:
Evaluation:

8 *Miscellaneous Ad*
Listening to evaluate advertising

Directions: One Saturday, Mr. and Mrs. Coleman were sitting at the kitchen table, drinking coffee. Mr. Coleman was thinking about growing some new flowers, both inside and outside of the house. As he browsed through the local shopping newspaper, he found an interesting ad which he read aloud to his wife.

You listen to the ad, too. See if you can find out why Mr. Coleman was interested in the ad, and see if you can find out why the ad writer put this ad in the newspaper. Here is the ad:

African Violets for Sale

I grow my own African Violets in my garden house right in my back yard. These violets bloom almost continually. Come to 7701 West Broadway for the prettiest African Violets you have ever seen — all kinds, all colors. Advice on the tender care and feeding of these plants is given also.

Mrs. Wilfred

Now, can you tell us why Mr. Coleman was interested in this ad? Why do you suppose Mrs. Wilfred put this ad in the paper?

Discussion:
Evaluation:

9 *Miscellaneous Ad*
Listening to evaluate advertising

Directions: Walking through the parking lot of a shopping center, Cheryl stooped down to pick up a folded piece of paper that had the word *Sale* written on it. "Hold on," she said to her little brother, Scott. As she picked up the paper, she started to read about the sale.

"Tell me, too," said Scott. So Cheryl began to read the sale ad that someone had written down on a piece of paper. You listen to the ad, too, and see if you can figure out why the ad was written. We'll talk about the reasons for holding this kind of sale. Here is the ad Cheryl read:

Garage Sale
September 15, 19XX
303 East 12th Street
8 a.m. to 5 p.m.

Women's clothes (sizes 10-16); infant's and children's clothes (sizes 2-6x); assorted sizes men's sports jackets and trousers. One dining room table with four chairs; one student's desk; one rocking chair; and several lamps. Various tools. Many other interesting odds and ends. Books and magazines, too.

What do you think the reasons might be for this kind of sale? Why do you suppose this kind of ad was just written out in someone's handwriting, rather than being printed in the newspaper as an ad?

Discussion:
Evaluation:

10 *Miscellaneous Ad*
Listening to evaluate advertising

Directions: Outside the local hardware store, Penny stopped to look at the bulletin board where everyone was invited to put up ads for things to sell, buy, and trade, or notices about special events. One ad was particularly interesting to Penny, for it told a pretty good story about a person who wanted to make a trade.

You listen to this ad to see if you can tell me why this person wants to make a trade, and why the ad was placed on the bulletin board.

Have Ski Equipment — Will Trade!
After some winter mishaps and several days in the hospital, I have decided to take up a hobby more suited to my athletic abilities. Complete girl's ski equipment available — skis, clamps, wax, the whole business. Boots (size 7) and three new girl's ski outfits (size 8). Will trade for modern stereo equipment in excellent condition. Call my parents.

Mr. and Mrs. S. Byars
498-7432

Why do you think this person wants to trade ski equipment for a stereo set? Could you figure out the story that led to this ad?

Discussion:
Evaluation:

11 Miscellaneous Ad
Listening to evaluate advertising

Directions: Mr. Jatta was looking through the ads in the shopping newspaper that was delivered to his door each week. One ad was very interesting and made him wish that, just this one time, he didn't live in a small apartment. He had always had pets and had loved them very much.

Here is the ad Mr. Jatta read. You see if you can tell something about the writer of the ad.

July 2, 19XX

Fella, our two-year-old Collie, needs a new home. We are moving to New Jersey and cannot take him along to live in a small apartment.

Fella is playful but very gentle with children. He loves a big yard to play in, and lots of people for company. He is a good watchdog.

We don't want any money for our dog; we just want to be sure he has a good home. We will be leaving for New Jersey in August. Please call us, the Jones family, at 669-7321, if you have the home and love that Fella needs. Then you can come over and meet our fine pet.

What can you tell about the writer of this ad? Why was this ad written?

Discussion:
Evaluation:

12 Commercial Advertisement
Listening to evaluate advertising

Directions: As Derek was reading an ad in the newspaper, he became so excited that he read the ad again, out loud, even though he was all by himself. Derek liked "Creamy Chew" candy bars very

much; he knew they cost 10¢ each. See if you can find out why Derek
was so excited about the ad.

Listen carefully and see if you can figure out why the ad was put
in the newspaper. The ad is very short:

Special Buy!

On November 11, 12, and 13, there will be a special sale on
"Creamy Chew" candy bars at the Big R Drug Store. "Creamy
Chew" candy bars will be on sale at six bars for 39¢ if you bring in
this coupon. Only one coupon per person.

Can you see why Derek was excited about the ad? Why do you
think the ad was put in the newspaper?

Discussion:
Evaluation:

13 *Commercial Advertisement*
Listening to evaluate advertising

Directions: Mr. Billings and his son, Todd, liked to camp out. One
evening when they were watching television, they heard a commercial that made them listen carefully.

You listen, also, to see why Mr. Billings and Todd were interested
in the commercial. Try to find out just what kind of commercial this
was. Here is the commercial:

Sale at Camping Store

On sale Friday and Saturday only! Our "Go Camping! Go Pack-
ing!" small tents will be on sale for $31.95. Check our last week's ads
because these small tents are regularly priced at $36.00. Save mon-
ey, and also get a good tent that has a 5′ X 7′ sleeping area — big
enough for two sleeping bags. These nylon tents, weighing only six
pounds, will be on sale Friday and Saturday only. So come to the
Camping Center, at the corner of Dallas and East Streets.

Why do you think that Mr. Billings and Todd were interested in
the TV commercial? Why do you think the Camping Center put this
commercial on television?

Discussion:
Evaluation:

14   *Commercial Advertisement*
Listening to evaluate advertising

Directions: In a truck and bus magazine, Jack was reading about a new line of trucks and busses that a manufacturing company was producing for other companies to buy. As Jack was interested in this ad, he took the magazine to his older sister, Liz, who was taking high school science classes. As he read the ad to Liz, Jack decided to think about the kind of ad it was and the reasons why this company was advertising its products. Here is the ad Jack read:

Our electric-powered engines have already been put to the test in busses and trucks. Several communities in our nation have battery-powered mail trucks. These communities have decided to use this kind of power because the engines are smog-free and cost only about one-tenth as much as gasoline-fueled trucks. Electric trucks used by the Postal Service are powered by two 36-volt batteries and have a top speed of 30 miles per hour. Every other night, the trucks are plugged into a charger so the batteries will be ready for work the next morning.

We were one of the several manufacturers who demonstrated our **electric buses and trucks in Yosemite National Park** last year. We feel that using electric busses to carry people around the valley floor helps them to see and hear the beauty of Yosemite. Traffic jams are eliminated; electric busses do not cause smog; and there is no more need for the loud noises of the regular gasoline-powered car or bus in this natural setting.

What kind of commercial advertisement do you think this is? Why do you think the company was advertising its products? Who would be interested in such an ad?

Discussion:
Evaluation:

15   *Commercial Advertisement*
Listening to evaluate advertising

Directions: Ben Dunkin and his wife were reading the Sunday paper when Ben said, "Say, listen to this ad! It tells all about how to brighten up the house — and for only $1.50!"

You listen to the ad and see if you think this $1.50 product alone could make all that difference in an apartment or a house.

No longer do you have to endure those long winter months in drab surroundings. The home owner or apartment dweller can brighten any room with a gorgeous, living, blooming geranium plant. Choose plants of one color, or select a rainbow of gorgeous colors that will bring sunshine and summer into any room, even if the temperature outside is below zero.

Our giant geraniums are spectacular and magnificent. Come in and see them growing in their 3 1/2-inch plastic pots. At only $1.50 a plant, preserve the best of spring and summer in your own home all year 'round.

Do you agree or disagree that this $1.50 plant could bring "spring and summer in your home all year 'round?"

Discussion:
Evaluation:

16 Commercial Advertisement
Listening to evaluate advertising

Directions: Henry called his friend Gilbert on the telephone. Laughing loudly, he read a newspaper ad to Gilbert, who often went fishing with him.

You listen to the ad that Henry read. See if you can see why the ad seemed so funny to Henry and Gilbert.

Catch more fish, better fish, and bigger fish. Our new, specially treated worms help you catch more fish whether you are fishing in a small pond, a rushing stream, or a big lake. Our special soil and feeding procedures make our worms so yummy to any fish. Fish just can't stand it until they capture our delectable worms. Come in and price our buckets of irresistible worms. They're worth the price when you find out that you can haul in limit catches of fish in no time!

Why do you think these fishermen thought the ad was funny?

Even if you don't know much about fishing, are there any aspects of this ad that seem funny to you?

Discussion:
Evaluation:

17   *Commercial Advertisement*
Listening to evaluate advertising

Directions: Carolyn liked her mother's cooking, especially the German chocolate cake she sometimes helped her mother bake. Carolyn always paid attention when she heard one particular commercial about a brand of chocolate, "Chocolate Triple C," that was supposed to be very, very good. Carolyn decided to call her mother in to listen when the ad came on again. She wanted to check if the ad was truthful in everything that was said.

You listen, too, and see if you could check on all the facts the announcer gives about "Chocolate Triple C."

Seventy-five per cent of the finest restaurants in the United States and Canada use our brand of chocolate, "Chocolate Triple C." "Chocolate Triple C" is great in tempting hot chocolate drinks, creamy chocolate pies, and sumptuous fudge toppings for ice cream and chocolate cakes. "Chocolate Triple C" costs a little more than the average chocolate, but we're sure that your family will love you for introducing them to our chocolate treat, "Chocolate Triple C."

The ad sounds tasty, doesn't it? What are some of the facts that tell how good that kind of chocolate is? Could you check all or some of these facts to see if they were true?

Discussion:
Evaluation:

18   *Commercial Advertisement*
Listening to evaluate advertising

Directions: Ms. Alice Jacobs heard a commercial on her car radio one morning as she was driving to work. While the announcer read the commercial, lively music was playing in the background. After Ms. Jacobs heard the commercial, which was about buying new clothes, she decided to go shopping during her lunch hour. Then she stopped to think. "There were so many interesting words in that clothes commercial. That's why I want to go shopping!"

Here is the commercial she heard. You listen for some of the special words that might make someone want to go shopping.

Y Brand clothes has something new for young career women! We have picked the newest colors for your spring wardrobe. The sun rises and sets in our new shades for you. After the long, drab winter, we have selected the warmest, softest, most vibrant colors especially with you in mind. Our colors have been taken from the sky, the earth, the sand, and the sea to give you their glowing, vibrant warmth. The sun rises and sets this spring in the new colors of Y Brand clothes.

What kinds of words did you hear that make the Y Brand clothes sound so attractive?

Discussion:
Evaluation:

19 Commercial Advertisement
Listening to evaluate advertising

Directions: Larry picked up the shopper's guide newspaper at his front door. He needed to buy some new supplies for the house. His attention was drawn to one particular ad in the center of the first page.

Here is the ad Larry read. Listen to find out what is being sold and how the ad is written to attract attention.

Our plastic trash cans are great!
Yes, sir, you bet they're strong!
Our factory's time for making them is long.
Yes, ma'am, they're pretty — get one tonight,
They come in yellow, red, purple, orange, and white.
Yes, indeed, they're a good deal,
You might even call them a steal!
Come in while the sale is on,
(They might not be here very long,
For they're selling out so very fast!)

> We're not sure they're going to last.
> $3.98 is really a blast!

What is for sale? What was the main way the product was being advertised? Were there any other gimmicks used to attract your attention?

Discussion:
Evaluation:

20 Commercial Advertisement
Listening to evaluate advertising

Directions: Mrs. Spangler heard a radio commercial about a baking dish which made her say to herself, "If a dish can do all that, I'd better buy one!"

You listen to the commercial, too, and then decide if you think Mrs. Spangler should buy the dish.

> Buy our latest baking dish which regularly sells for $1.75 but is on sale this week for just 87¢. Your cooking will improve. The children will love your moist, delightful meatloaf, and your neighbors will gasp at the sight of your fluffy cakes. Your husband will call for seconds of your eye-catching, tummy-pleasing pies. You can't go wrong!

Do you think Mrs. Spangler believed all the wonderful things the ad said would happen if she bought the baking dish? Would you? What did the commercial claim would happen with the purchase of the baking dish?

Discussion:
Evaluation:

21 Commercial Advertisement
Listening to evaluate advertising

Directions: Maria and Eleanor were comparing ads in the newspaper, trying to find interesting ones to take to school. They were looking for ads that made rather dull products sound exciting. Suddenly, Maria said, "Here's a good one!"

You listen along with Eleanor to find out why this ad is so interesting.

Are you in the market for some rugged rope for a rugged he-man job? We have ropes of all kinds, for every use. Stout rope will stretch a clothesline so that the wash won't drag the ground; even stouter rope will stretch your kid's sagging tent in the back yard. Rope, clothesline, string, twine, and cord will answer all your sagging, drooping, and stringing rope needs.

Rope and clothesline are not really very exciting subjects. But were there any particular words or groups of words used in this ad that helped make rope, clothesline, and cord a little more interesting?

Discussion:
Evaluation:

22 Commercial Advertisement
Listening to evaluate advertising

Directions: Mrs. Banks was watching television when she heard a commercial about a new furniture store in town. As the announcer told about the store, many kinds of furniture and furniture groupings were shown on television. Mrs. Banks listened carefully to the announcer to hear what he was saying and to see how he was trying to get people to the new store to take a look at the merchandise.

You listen to the message and try to discover how the new store owners are trying to attract customers.

Come in to see our new showroom full of the newest furniture you could find under one roof. The Furniture Shop invites you to come and browse. Bring the children and the neighbors (but, please, leave the family dog at home). Come as you are—barefoot, with rollers in your hair, or on your way home after work. We just want you to see the many furniture offerings we have at The Furniture Shop.

How are the new store owners trying to get people into their store? Did the announcer say anything to make people feel welcome?

Discussion:
Evaluation:

23 Commercial Advertisement
Listening to evaluate advertising

Directions: "I can't believe it," said Mel after reading an ad to his dad. Mel's family needed a new lawn mower, and he and his parents had been out looking at different models of mowers.

This is the ad Mel read. You listen and see if you agree with Mel's statement, "I can't believe it."

Easy to care for, simple to use, and just the kind of mower a person such as you would want. You sit on a cushioned driver's seat and steer with ease, and that tall grass on your property immediately turns into a velvety, well-cared for green lawn that looks as if you had spent hours working on it. Call us now for a free demonstration.

Do you agree or disagree with Mel? Have you ever mowed a lawn? Is it as easy as the ad says it is? Would you buy the lawn mower right away?

Discussion:
Evaluation:

24 Commercial Advertising
Listening to evaluate advertising

Directions: In Room 11, the fifth grade students were evaluating a television commercial that several of them had seen. They wrote down three questions that they wanted the other boys and girls to answer after they heard the commercial. The commercial was about a new breakfast cereal. Here are the questions:

1. How might mothers feel about this commercial?

2. Are there any reasons why people should eat breakfast?

3. Do children get low grades because they don't eat this particular cereal?

Now you listen to the commercial so that you can participate in a discussion as these children planned.

Attention, mothers! Do your children get the "drags" or "blahs" at school? In the mornings, do you think they may be missing out on math or reading lessons because of poor diets? Boys and girls who are bringing home *D*'s and *F*'s on their report cards may need *Breakfast Tuneup*, our new breakfast cereal. *Breakfast Tuneup* has more nutritional value than any other breakfast cereal on the market. Because it is also the fastest selling cereal, shouldn't you be a good mother and give your child the very best breakfast available?

Now, let's try to answer those three questions.

Discussion:

Evaluation:

25 Commercial Advertisement
Listening to evaluate advertising

Directions: Mr. Murphy was laughing at a television commercial when his teenage daughter, Laurie, walked in the room. "You'll like this commercial. It's a funny one!" said Mr. Murphy. Laurie started watching the commercial, and soon they were both laughing. The commercial showed a strong, healthy, middle-aged man who said he had found the way to health.

As you listen, ask yourself if this man's health program would be a good one for all men of his age.

Many people tell me that I look as young as my sons. Frankly, a man who is over forty can feel dragged down at times. Several years ago, I found myself feeling tired all the time. I yelled at the kids when I got home from work and complained about things in general to my wife. One day, my wife showed me an ad in the newspaper telling about a special program at the UFF Gym. The program was designed especially for tired business executives.

Well, after three months at the gym, I felt like a new man. I have a special diet. I go jogging every morning, and I work out at the UFF Gym three evenings a week.

Everyone says I'm a changed man! Think I'd change my UFF Gym program now? Not on your life!

What do you think about this commercial? Would this program be a good one for all people over forty? Is the man in the commercial an actor, or a person who actually takes the gym program?

Discussion:

Evaluation:

26 *Commercial Advertisement*
Listening to evaluate advertising

Directions: Mr. and Mrs. Williams were talking about an ad they read in a magazine. Their guests, the Campbells, wanted to hear the ad, too, so Mrs. Williams read it out loud. The Williams felt the ad was not truthful about the toys it was describing. Listen to the ad, then decide whether or not you think the ad is believable.

Parents, do you want your child to have a good start in school? "Toys by Us" are the toys for you. Our company prepares your two-, three-, and four-year-olds to learn how to count, say the alphabet, and read newspaper headlines before starting to school.

Here are some letters from happy parents:

Dear "Toys by Us" Company,
Thanks to you, my three-year-old daughter is teaching her six-year-old sister how to read. We love "Toys by Us."

> Mrs. M. K.
> Chicago

Dear Company that makes "Toys by Us,"
Your number games are terrific. After having gone through Game 6 of Numbers by "Toys by Us," my five-year-old son is now in charge of distributing the milk money, lunch money, and weekly allowances to his four older brothers and sisters.

> Mr. and Mrs. E. L. B.
> San Francisco

Do you think the ad is believable? Why or why not?

Discussion:
Evaluation:

Part 4
Checking the Facts

Listening to conversation is an everyday occurrence. We spend a good deal of time chatting with friends, and in doing so, we express our opinions and listen to the opinions of others. We thus come to know the likes and dislikes of our friends and colleagues, and they come to know ours. It is important that children, too, learn that we all have personal likes and dislikes, and that interests vary from person to person.

Beyond conversation, children need to learn how to listen evaluatively and critically to speakers. Because speech is transitory, it places more demands on the listener than does writing. The listener must learn to ask himself these questions:

1. Who is doing the talking?
2. What is the purpose of his speech?
3. Does the speaker know his subject?
4. What is the speaker's point of view?
5. Can his facts be verified?

While previous parts of this book have emphasized reading and math, the listening activities in Part 4 will fit in well as part of the social studies curriculum. In this part, the children will learn how to evaluate the motives of a speaker. Sample conversations help them learn that others may have points of view different from theirs. Examples of TV, radio, and newspaper editorials and headlines help bring out this point. Other listening experiences are designed to help them probe the veracity of the speaker. Activities that call for the use of basic reference tools conclude Part 4.

1   Conversation
    Listening to interpret a speaker's point of view

Directions: Here is a short conversation that was overheard at a science fair. You listen to the two girls and see if you can find out what one special interest of each girl might be. Afterwards, we'll talk about why the girls decided to look at different displays.

> Girl #1: Let's go over to that display that demonstrates the uses of electricity. In the newspaper last night, I read that the girl who worked on the project won a prize for developing a computer powered by electricity.
>
> Girl #2: While you're looking at that project, I'll be right across the aisle. There's an egg-hatching project over there. I'm going to visit my uncle this summer, and he has a hatchery. I'd better learn a little about how eggs are hatched.

Can you determine why the girls were interested in different projects at the science fair? Can you remember any comments made by either girl which told you why she was interested in a certain project?

Discussion:
Evaluation:

2   Conversation
    Listening to interpret a speaker's point of view

Directions: As they walked home from school, two boys were talking about their favorite kinds of books. You listen to their conversation and see if you can find out what their interests are.

> Boy #1: I'm going to the library this afternoon to borrow another Andre Norton book. I really like science fiction. I've read *Key Out of Time,* and I need to return *Night of Masks.* I plan to read everything Norton has written.
>
> Boy #2: Not me! I'm an outdoor adventure fan. One of my favorites is *My Side of the Mountain*—it's a human survival story. Another great book is *Incident at Hawk's Hill.* *

*Andre Norton, *Key Out of Time* (Cleveland: World, 1963), and *Night of Masks* (New York: Harcourt, 1964); Jean George, *My Side of the Mountain* (New York: Dutton, 1959); and Allan Eckert, *Incident at Hawk's Hill* [Boston: Little, 1971).

Can you tell now just what these boys' different interests are? Both like to read, but what are their favorite kinds of books?

Discussion:
Evaluation:

3 Conversation
Listening to interpret a speaker's point of view

Directions: Two girls were talking on the playground about bicycles and bicycle paths. As you listen to a part of their conversation, see if you can figure out why each girl feels the way she does about bicycles and bicycle paths.

Girl #1: I used to have a bike, but we sold it because there wasn't any place to ride it where we moved. The freeway off-ramp is close to our house, so it's too dangerous to ride in the street.

Girl #2: My mom and sister and I ride our bikes a lot to the shopping center. We ride in the bicycle path that's just been made. Come over to my house whenever you want and you can borrow my sister's bike. We'll ride over to the shopping center, and I'll show you the bicycle path.

Can you tell why each girl feels the way she does about bicycling? What were some comments that helped you figure out their points of view?

Discussion:
Evaluation:

4 Conversation
Listening to interpret a speaker's point of view

Directions: Listen carefully to a small portion of a conversation that two boys were having in the cafeteria at school. Yes, they were talking about food. Listen to the conversation and see if you can understand why each boy said what he did.

Boy #1: Oh, boy! I've got fresh strawberries in my lunchbox today.

I'm sure glad when strawberry season rolls around. I could eat a ton of them. Want a couple?

Boy #2:   Wow! Strawberries are good, but I have to eat them cooked. If I eat them raw, I get hives in half an hour. My mom makes them into strawberry jam, and you should taste the delicious strawberry sundaes and shortcakes we make with cooked strawberries.

Do you know a little bit more about each boy now? What did they say about strawberries that made them different?

Discussion:

Evaluation:

5   *Conversation*
Listening to interpret a speaker's point of view

Directions: Two boys were talking outside the school gate one morning about the games they like to play. As you listen to a part of their conversation, see if you can tell what games each boy likes to play.

Boy #1:   I like to play checkers, chess, and backgammon with one of my older brothers and sisters. Sometimes at night my whole family plays different kinds of card games.

Boy #2:   I don't have any brothers or sisters, but I have a lot of friends my own age. We play baseball, shoot baskets, and ride our bikes most of the time.

What kind of games did the first boy prefer? The second boy? Did they each like the same kinds of games?

Discussion:

Evaluation:

6   *Newspaper Editorials*
Listening to interpret headlines

Directions: Mr. Gerard was talking about community problems with his class in Room 31. The students knew that the city council held meetings to discuss these problems, but they knew, too, that often there was no one right answer. Everyone agreed, however, that it was important to know the point of view of speakers in a discussion.

Then Mr. Gerard said, "One way of bringing out a person's point of view is through a newspaper editorial or radio or television commentary. Have you ever been listening to the news when the announcer said he was going to give an editorial comment? Newspaper readers can show their points of view, too, by writing letters to the editor."

Mr. Gerard explained, "Just by reading the headlines of a newspaper editorial, we can sometimes get a clue about the writer's point of view. I'm going to read some examples of editorial headlines to you. The headlines will come in pairs. Listen for differences in their points of view."

You can listen, too, as Mr. Gerard reads his examples.

1. Cast a *No* Vote on Proposition A
   Proposition A Requires a *Yes* Vote

2. New Band Uniforms Greatly Needed
   Use School Money for Essentials—Not Uniforms

3. Park Statue is Work of Art
   Should We Pay for Car Wreck in Park?

4. "New Dam Unnecessary," Say Hiking Enthusiasts
   New Dam Needed for More Water Storage

5. Traffic Guard Needed at Dangerous Intersections
   "Install Traffic Signals," says Safety Committee

6. More Trains, Buses, and Subways Needed
   We Need Wider Highways and More Freeways

Discussion:
Evaluation:

7 *Sports Headlines*
Listening to interpret headlines

Directions: Do you ever read the sports section of the newspaper or listen to sports news on radio or TV? Headlines of sports stories can indicate a point of view, too, just like headlines of editorials. Here are some examples of sports headlines. As I read them, see if you can determine their point of view. We'll discuss them one at a time.

1. You are a friend of Fred, who is a great runner and track star. But at a track meet one Saturday, Fred didn't win even one event. On Monday, the school paper had this headline: "Flying Fred Flubs." How would you imagine Fred felt after reading this? As his friend, how would you feel?

2. Imagine that you are a reporter for the Jackson High School newspaper. You are covering a big football game against Wilson High School. Jackson wins! Which headline would you probably use?
     Wilson High Narrowly Loses
     Jackson High Trounces Wilson

3. Imagine that you attend all of Dudley University's basketball games because you think the team is great. Then, one Friday night, Dudley loses to Green University. Which of the following headlines best shows your point of view?
     Green U. Conquers Dudley U.
     Dudley U. Valiently Loses to Green U.

4. You have just read two stories about a prize fight in two different papers. Both stories said that Louie won and Wally lost. Listen to the two headlines and see if you can tell whether the writers had the same or different points of view:
     Louis KO's Wally in the 4th!
     "Bad Luck" says Wally: Vows to fight Louie Again

5. On two different radio stations, you heard two sportscasters tell about a baseball game in which Cochise High School beat Williams High School. Do these headlines show different points of view?
     Cochise High School Batters Trip Williams
     Williams High Team Still has Chance for the Crown

Discussion:
Evaluation:

8 *Subject Area Specialists*
Listening to ascertain the speaker's qualifications

Directions: In Room 15, Miss Carsten asked her class to think about all the special interests different people have. Some of us like to learn about space travel, others ride horses, some play guitar. People have many hobbies besides their main jobs, and that's good.

"But right now," said Miss Carsten, "let's think about people's main jobs. We're going to think of people who are authorities in their fields—people we would turn to if we needed to find out some specific information. I'm going to name three people in different occupations, then you can decide which of them might be the best person to talk about a specific subject."

You listen, too, as Miss Carsten reads these examples and see if you can help answer the questions.

1. Here are some people who perform different kinds of jobs:

   an artist   a butcher   a grocery clerk

   Who could best demonstrate how to cut a side of beef?

2. Here are three other workers:

   a coal miner   a librarian   a jeweler

   Who could tell us about the differences between real diamonds and imitation ones?

Continue the listening activity in this manner, first listing several occupations, then asking a question that only one of them is clearly able to answer. Additional examples include:

3. bank cashier   computer specialist   highway engineer

   Who could tell us how best to prevent problems involving vote counting if an election is being handled by computers?

4. driving training instructor   rancher   salesman

   Which of these people could tell us how to learn how to avoid traffic accidents?

5. poet   librarian   mayor

   Who might be the best resource person in helping us learn to use the card catalog in the library?

6. bus driver   teacher   lawyer

   Who could tell us about how laws help protect citizens?

7. electrician   lumberjack   furniture maker

   Which one of these people might best be able to talk to us on the topic, "Cutting Timber in the High Country?"

8. teacher   airline pilot   shoe repairman

   Which of these people would be willing and able to discuss the changes in commercial air flights from 1956 to 1976?

9. coal miner   farmer   truck driver

   Who could tell us about the need for providing safe mine shafts?

10. car mechanic   nurse   electrician

    Who would be best qualified to speak on the topic, "Keeping the Accident Victim Quiet while Waiting for the Ambulance?"

11. plumber   swimming champion   dentist

    Which person could give the best advice about the location of a swimming pool and the showers, so that the water pipes would be in the proper place?

12. dentist   teacher   city councilman

    Which one of these persons could talk to our class about the major causes of tooth decay?

13. dance instructor   sales clerk   folksinger

    Which person might best be able to demonstrate the music and musical instruments used in the Appalachians through the years?

(*Note:* In this section, you'll no doubt have many reactions, such as, "My mother drives a school bus, and she used to be a nurse. She plays a guitar and sings folk songs, too!" Encourage these comments showing the many interests and abilities one person can have. Remind the class, however, that in these examples only the occupations of the people were given.)

Discussion:
Evaluation:

9 *Checking the Facts about Teachers
Listening to evaluate source material*

Directions: The teacher, Mr. Willis, was discussing the duties of a teacher with his class as part of a study about careers. Mr. Willis said, "I have a notice about teachers that I'm going to read to you.

Listen carefully, because it may surprise you. It shows just how important the date of writing of any book, law, or advertisement can be."

You listen, too, as Mr. Willis reads "The Duties and Responsibilities of a Teacher." Here is the notice:

Teachers are to clean the school room carefully at the end of each day. After sweeping the floor with the broom, coal is to be brought in. The coal bucket is to be placed next to the stove so that the teacher will be ready to start the fire early the next morning before the students arrive.

Male and female teachers are to behave with decorum during their out-of-school hours. They are to attend church on Sundays. Female teachers must live in boarding houses approved by the Board of Education. No female teacher is to marry. Upon marriage of a female teacher, her teaching career is terminated.

When Mr. Willis finished reading the notice, he told the class, "There is one more thing I need to tell you. This is the kind of notice that was given to many teachers in our state in 1875. Do you think dates are important when you read or hear a notice?"

Now that we have heard the notice, what do you think?

Discussion:
Evaluation:

10 Checking the Facts about Postage
Listening to evaluate source material

Directions: Bill seemed to be very confused as he read aloud some information in the *World Almanac*. To help clear up this confusion, Bill's friend Gene found another *World Almanac* that had a different publishing date.

Listen as I read the conversation that Bill and Gene had. As you listen, see if you can discover why the year a book was published is important when you want to look up certain facts.

Bill: In *The World Almanac and Book of Facts*, listen to what I just learned about the cost of mailing letters today:

  First Class Postal Rates
  Domestic
  Valid in the United States, Territories, Possessions

> Letters—6¢ per ounce or fraction thereof
> Postal cards—5¢ each
> Air mail letters—10¢ per ounce or fraction thereof; limit
> 7 ounces.

Gene: Now, we know that's not right. Let me see that book. Why, Bill, you have the 1970 *World Almanac*. Let's see what the 1973 *World Almanac* says. I'll read it to you:

> First Class Postal Rates
> Domestic
> Valid in the United States, Territories, Possessions
> Letters—8¢ per ounce or fraction thereof
> Postal cards—6¢ each
> Air mail letters—11¢ per ounce or fraction thereof; limit
> 8 ounces.

Bill, you need to have the latest information. You had the "right" information but for the "wrong" year! The price of mailing letters has gone up since 1970. We had better look in the most recent *Almanac* to find out what it is now.

What did Gene mean when he said Bill had "the right information for the wrong year?" In what ways does the date of a book of facts seem to be important? Who would like to check this fact in our almanac?

Discussion:
Evaluation:

11   Checking the Facts about the Census
Listening to evaluate source material

Directions: Betsy and Gil were working on a report about the five largest cities in the United States. They decided from their reading that New York City was the largest city in the United States, but they disagreed on the size of that city. Betsy said that according to the U.S. Bureau of the Census, 10,694,633 people lived there. Gil reported that the U.S. Bureau of the Census had counted 11,528,649 people. Because Betsy and Gil got different numbers from the same source, they turned to their teacher, Mrs. Medina, for help. This is what she told them. Listen to find out why the date of publication of a book of facts is so important:

Your facts are both correct, Betsy and Gil. They both are taken from the U.S. Bureau of Census which counts the number of people in the U.S. every ten years. Both of you got your information from the *World Almanac*, which is a good source. Betsy, however, got her information from a 1965 *World Almanac*, which gave the results of the 1960 census. Gil's information came from the 1972 *World Almanac*, which gives the census for 1970. Gil has the most recent information about the official count of the people in New York City.

Now that you and Betsy and Gil have heard Mrs. Medina's explanation, why do you think the date of a book of facts makes such a big difference? Who would like to check this fact in our *World Almanac?*

Discussion:
Evaluation:

12 *Checking the Facts about the U.N.*
Listening to evaluate source material

Directions: Jackie was preparing a report on the United Nations. She had taken some notes, and now she was putting her notes in order. She saw that two notes disagreed. Jackie decided to read them aloud to herself so she could tell what was wrong.

As Jackie reviews her notes, you listen, too. See if you can find out why her notes disagree. This is what she read:

Note #1: As of September, 1969, there were 126 member nations in the U.N. (*World Almanac*, 1970 edition).
Note #2: As of October, 1971, there were 130 member nations in the U.N. (*World Almanac*, 1972 edition).
"Now I see," said Jackie. "The number of member nations changes. Four new countries were added between September, 1969, and October, 1971. I had better hunt up some more recent information. There may be even more member nations in the U.N. today."

Did you figure out why Jackie's two notes disagreed? Why did she decide to look up the same information in a more recent edition of the *World Almanac?* Who would like to check this fact in our *World Almanac?*

Discussion:
Evaluation:

13   *Checking the Facts about Israel
Listening to evaluate source material*

Directions: Alex was looking in an atlas for a map of Israel. He looked and looked, but he couldn't find that country any place in the Middle East. Alex decided to ask his friend, Boyd, if he had found a map showing Israel.

You listen to their conversation, too, and see if you can help Alex solve his problem.

Boyd: Yes, I found a map of Israel in the atlas.
Alex: But I have an atlas, too, and there's no map of Israel in the Middle East.
Boyd: Let me see your atlas. . . . Do you know what? You really have an old book here. Its publication date is 1953, but Israel didn't become a nation until four years later! You'd better use my atlas. It's more up-to-date.

How did Boyd help Alex solve his problem? Why is it important that we use source materials that have the most recent publication dates? Who would like to check this fact in our atlas?

Discussion:
Evaluation:

14   *Checking the Facts about Maps
Listening to evaluate source materials*

Directions: Mr. Yoshida and his class were talking about the moon and about moon exploration. I'm going to read part of their conversation to you. As you listen, try to remember two reasons why maps are important for exploring and learning about new places. Here is what Mr. Yoshida said:

For centuries, people on earth knew nothing more about the

moon than what they could see from the earth on clear nights. After the invention of the telescope, people learned that there were craters—deep holes on the moon which from the earth looked like the dark spots we sometimes call the man in the moon. Larger telescopes helped us learn more about the physical features of the moon's surface. Cameras aboard early unmanned U.S. space flights took even closer pictures of the moon's surface. From these pictures, maps were made. Good maps were needed for the Apollo missions so the astronauts could land in the exact spots that scientists had chosen. We even have pictures of the back side of the moon which were taken from command modules which orbited the moon while our astronauts explored the moon's surface.

Who wants to check our atlas to see if it has a picture of the dark side of the moon? Why do you think accurate maps are necessary, especially in exploring new places, such as the moon?

Discussion:
Evaluation:

15 Checking the Facts about Barbados
Listening to evaluate source materials

Directions: Libby was looking in the encyclopedia for a picture of the flag of Barbados, an island country in the Caribbean. As you listen to her conversation with Steve, see if you can figure out why she couldn't find a picture of that flag in her encyclopedia.

Libby: I've looked under B for Barbados, and I found some information about the country, but I can't find a picture of the flag. The encyclopedia says that in 1958 Barbados was not self-governing.

Steve: I bet I know the problem. Let's check the publication date of that encyclopedia set. . . . It's only good up to 1959, the year it was published. Anything that happed after 1959 won't be in it. Let's look in this new encyclopedia under B. Here's Barbados, and here's the flag—it's yellow and purple. This encyclopedia says that Barbados became an independent country in 1966.

Why was the date important in Libby's problem? Who would

like to check our encyclopedia and see if it has a picture of the flag of Barbados?

Discussion:
Evaluation:

16 Checking the Facts about the U.S.
Listening to evaluate source material

Directions: Carol and Frank were working on a social studies assignment about the United States. Frank wanted to find out which were the first 25 states admitted to the Union, and Carol wanted to find out which were the last 25 states to be admitted. They had two sets of encyclopedias, published in different years. Listen to part of their conversation and see if you can understand why one of them used the old set, and the other one the new set.

Frank: I'll use this old encyclopedia. Under *U*, I can look up *United States of America*. It has a list showing the date each state was admitted.
Carol: You can't use that old book! The publication date is 1953. We'd better share this new set of encyclopedias.
Frank: I already know that the twenty-fifth state was Arkansas, and it was admitted in 1863. This old set of encyclopedias will still give me the right information.

Why do you suppose Frank could use the older set of encyclopedias? What does this discussion tell you about some of the facts in older reference books? Who wants to check our encyclopedias to find out when the most recent state was admitted to the United States?

Discussion:
Evaluation:

17 Checking the Facts about Money
Listening to evaluate source materials

Directions: Walt, Renee, and Pam went to their teacher, Mrs. Pederman, and Walt said, "We have a report for you, Mrs. Pederman. It's entitled, 'Time Changes All Things.' Would you like to hear it?"

As the children read their report, you listen, too. Pay attention to the reference books they used and see if the publication dates are important to their report.

Walt: Renee and I were trying to find out what kind of money is used in England. We used an encyclopedia with a publication date of 1969. We read that in 1966, there were approximately 280 pence in a pound. Then, the article said that after devaluation of the pound, there were only 240 pence in a pound.

Pam: Then I found a 1972 supplement edition to the encyclopedia that said England adopted a decimal system in 1972. Now there are 100 pence in a pound. So we decided to tell you these facts and call our report, "Time Changes All Things."

Do you think the children's oral report had a good title? Would the information they found in the 1969 encyclopedia have been enough to show the change in English money? Who wants to check our encyclopedia to see how many pence there are in a pound today?

Discussion:
Evaluation:

18 *Checking the Facts about Words*
Listening to evaluate source material

Directions: Mrs. Willsey was talking to her class about dictionaries. She explained about classroom dictionaries that have the most useful and common words in them for school use, and the huge, unabridged dictionaries that have many of the less common words in them. Then Mrs. Willsey pointed out that the publication date of a dictionary is also very important. Here is what she said:

New words are always being formed in our language, and eventually they get into dictionaries. Sometimes words that have had only one or two meanings for many years suddenly acquire new meanings. I have some questions to ask you about words. The first two have to do with words that were made up to fit new needs;

1. The word *megaton* is a unit of nuclear energy that measures energy in millions of tons of TNT. This unit of energy was developed after the first explosions of the hydrogen bomb in 1951 and 1952. Would you find the word *megaton* in a dictionary published in 1944, or in a dictionary published after 1954?

2. *Sputnik I* is a term found in unabridged dictionaries. This word entered our language after Russian scientists orbited the first spaceship around the earth. The one passenger on that 1957 flight was a dog. Would you find the word *Sputnik* in a 1953 dictionary, a 1955 dictionary, or a 1960 dictionary?

Then Mrs. Willsey discussed another aspect of language. You listen again to see if you can help her class with their study of the changing meanings of words.

3. You have all used the atlas, a reference book that is filled with maps and is helpful in our social studies lessons. If we look up the word *atlas* in the dictionary, we find several meanings. One of the oldest meanings of the word is a man's name. According to a Greek myth, Atlas was a giant who supported the heavens on his shoulders. Can you see any connection between this myth and the atlas we use in the classroom?

4. Apollo was a Greek and a Roman hero, a sky god who carried the sun to the sky every morning in his chariot. The word *Apollo* was chosen as the name of the manned U.S. space flights to the moon. These flights were called *Apollo* missions. Why do you suppose this name was chosen?

5. A word doesn't have to be long, complicated, or hard to pronounce to have a number of meanings. I'm going to give you a few minutes to think about the short word *run.* Keep track of the meanings you can think of, then we'll check the dictionary to see if there might be some we've forgotten.

Discussion:
Evaluation:

19   *Checking the Facts about Reference Books*
   Listening to evaluate source material

Directions: Kate and Mel had been working on a quiz for the rest of the class to answer. Their topic was, "Where Can You Find the Answer?" You listen to their questions, then we'll try to answer them one at a time.

Kate: We have a quiz for you today. It's called "Where Can You Find the Answer?"

Mel: Kate and I will take turns reading the questions. Before we read each question, though, we'll give you some choices of reference materials or people. After we read the question, you tell us which one would be most likely to have the answer.

1. encyclopedia   radio   dictionary

   Jim wanted to know who won the local basketball game last night. What source could help him?

2. newspaper   *World Almanac*   encyclopedia

   Mrs. Humphrey wanted to know how the stock market had gone that day. Where should she look for the answer?

3. encyclopedia   atlas   newspaper

   Joanne needed to find out what action had been taken at the city council yesterday for her report on city government. What source could help her best?

4. television news   encyclopedia   dictionary

   Darrell heard his mother say that there was a flood in the state where his grandmother lived. What source could tell Darrell exactly where that flood was?

5. radio   reference librarian   encyclopedia

   Mr. Arnold wanted to subscribe to a certain magazine, but he didn't know how much a subscription would cost, or where to write for one. Where should he go for the answer to his question?

Discussion:
Evaluation:

20   *Checking the Facts about Sierra Leone*
      Listening to evaluate source material

Directions: Brenda was working at a listening station in her classroom. She put on her earphones, and arranged an atlas, a *World Almanac*, and a dictionary on the table in front of her. She had a piece of paper and a pencil ready, too. The title on her paper read "Sierra Leone." Brenda wrote her name on the paper, then turned on the tape recording to hear her assignment.

As she listens, you listen, too, to see if you could follow the instructions. This is what the tape recording said:

Our class is about to begin a study of Africa. Your assignment is to find out two items about Sierra Leone, which is one of the independent countries in Africa.

The first question is this: Find a map of Africa using either the atlas, the *World Almanac*, or the dictionary. When you find a map that shows Sierra Leone, write down the name of the book in which you found the map and its page number, so you can show the map to the rest of the class later on.

Here is the second question: Write down the names of the countries and the body of water that surround Sierra Leone. Use any of the reference books on the table that you need.

Now if you were given this assignment, which reference books would you use? Who wants to check the facts in our reference books?

Discussion:
Evaluation:

21 *Checking the Facts about Sierra Leone*
Listening to evaluate source materials

Directions: Joey was sitting at a listening station, ready to go to work. He had reference books, papers, and a pencil on his table. As he turned on the tape recorder, this is what he heard. You listen along with Joey to see if you could follow the instructions.

Our class is going to study Africa this week. You can help by finding out some facts about Sierra Leone, which is one of the independent countries in Africa. Here is the first question: Using the atlas, the *World Almanac*, or the dictionary, find a short summary of the history of Sierra Leone.

1. When did Sierra Leone become a republic? Write down the

date and the name of the reference book used to locate this information. Put down the page number, too.

2. What is the capital of Sierra Leone? Write down this city's name, the title of the reference book that gave you the information, and the page number you found it on.

If you had this assignment, which book or books would you use? Who wants to check the books you've suggested to see if they give us that information?

Discussion:
Evaluation:

22 Checking the Facts about Sierra Leone
Listening to evaluate source materials

Directions: Kathy was interested in the country of Sierra Leone, and she was pleased that she had been given a special assignment to introduce this African nation to the class. Her papers and some reference books were on the table. Kathy adjusted her earphones and turned on the tape recorder.

You listen to Kathy's assignment and figure out which reference books would help her most.

We are beginning our study of Africa with the country of Sierra Leone, one of the republics of Africa. You may use the atlas, the *World Almanac*, or the dictionary to answer your question about Sierra Leone. Your question has three parts. Here it is: Using the reference books on your desk, look up the meanings of some of the products—the exports—that Sierra Leone sends to the rest of the world. These three products are: industrial diamonds, iron ore, and bauxite.

You will find only short definitions of these products in the reference book you select. As you find each definition, write it down, giving the name of the reference book and the page number. Your work will help the whole class as we study more about these products.

What book or books would you choose to help you answer these questions? Who wants to check them to see if you're right?

Discussion:
Evaluation: